My New Starts Now!

A Daily Devotional

By Vioree Brandon

Dedication

I would like to begin by thanking God for His unfailing love towards me, for keeping me when I didn't want to be kept, and for guiding me through this journey called life. I couldn't have made it without Jesus my Lord and Savior.

To my children, John R. Washington, Jaida C. Washington, Camille Cole Brandon and Aleah Curniffe, I love you all dearly. To my birth parents, Mr. & Mrs. Mitchell, thank you for making the decision to bring me into this world. We all have a purpose to fulfil here on earth; you took the step of allowing me to fulfill that purpose for which I am grateful. RIP Crystal Lynn Pool, Mom. To the women who raised me and helped me through the storms of growing up without a birth mother Hazel, Rose, Hattie, and Aunt Jennie, I love you all. A special thank you for embedding in me the foundation of Christ and for being examples of virtuous women. Thank you for showing me what true STRENGTH looks like. To all my sisters and brothers who have STUCK IT OUT with me, I know I am not easy at times, but I thank God for your patience. To Randi, Cherith, Telly, Tyrone, Edward, Vinity (RIP Baby Brother), Nittsa, Kernessa, Lee, Doug, Tammy, Danielle, Renay, and Natile, I love you guys. We may not speak every day, but you are always in my heart. Thank you, Omar, for helping me step by step through this process.

To my covering, my parents in the faith, Bishop Robert Rochford Sr. and Pastor Lois Elaine Rochford. Thank you for covering me, protecting, correcting, and keeping it all the way real with me, all the time. For acknowledging my weaknesses and my strengths and pushing me from my seat of comfort to a place of awesomeness. I salute you.

To my spiritual parents, Pastor Mark and Vanessa Dance, Elders William and Lily Pointer, Pastor Alvin Freeland, Lady (Mom) Mary Freeland, Bishop James Jones and Lady Joyce Jones, Prophet Walter Holmes, and Pastor Anita O'Brien: Thank you for pouring into me the WISDOM OF GOD. Thank you for loving me unconditionally, inspiring me, and charging me to move forward without allowing hindrances to stop me. I love you.

To Chee-Chee My Sweet Love, I sit here at my desk with tears in my eyes, reflecting on the life we shared together. As I went through the process of writing this book, I heard your voice, saying, *"I'm proud of you, keep going, don't stop, you can do it."* I will never forget all that you've taught me, the times you encouraged me by echoing I can't give up. The stamp of your unconditional love for me will be sealed on the tables of my heart. You will be forever missed. *Signed ~ Love*

Contents

Forward

"For someone who lives on milk is still an infant and doesn't know how to do what is right. Solid food is for those who are mature, who through training have the skill to recognize the difference between right and wrong." Hebrews 5:13-14NLT

To plainly state the truth contained in this scripture, the only reason why we don't grow and mature in our spiritual lives is because we don't use the truth we know. Our salvation is more than a destination; it is also a journey. We are admonished in 2 Peter 3:18 to grow in Grace and the knowledge of Jesus Christ. In the pages of this book Vioree Brandon has included practical daily devotions that will clearly lead you towards a fruitful life of spiritual growth and maturity. Reading, meditating, and acting upon each daily instruction will exercise your spirituality, deepen your relationships, and increase your ability to be used by God.

Read on and be blessed!

Rev William D. Pointer Jr.

Preface

In the Beginning...

Greetings, I would like to introduce you to your new beginning!

Say hello to a new day, a new experience, and a NEW YOU!
As you read each page, have a pen in hand, your heart and mind open to receive what God has to say to you. Write it down, yes, write it down! Then you will be able to look back over your notes to see how God has done a new work in you.

"If any man is in Christ, He is a new creation; old things have passed away; behold, all things have become new." 2 Corinthians 5:17

I love the Message version of this verse because it really breaks down your decision to become new in Christ.

"*Because of this decision, we don't evaluate people by what they have or how they look. We looked at the Messiah that way once and got it all wrong, as you know. We certainly don't look at him that way anymore. Now we look inside, and what we see is that anyone united with the Messiah gets a fresh start, is created new. The old life is gone: a new life burgeons! Look at it!*" 2 Corinthians 5:17 (MSG):

This scripture clearly explains how we should embrace our new life in Christ. So, look within yourself and see the beautiful person God has created on purpose and for a divine reason.

As you read this book, allow the words to filter your soul. My prayer is that as God creates the new you, He will give you a new way of thinking, a new talk, a new walk, a new outlook on life, and a new attitude. I pray this book reminds you daily that you are royalty. Whatever you face in your life, you are not alone. God is right there to plant you on solid ground. You will not sink; you are a winner. Read with surety that our daddy in heaven has you in the palm of His hands. Open your heart and set your mind to keep pressing forward.

"Your New Starts Right Now"

Be encouraged,

Minister Vioree Brandon

I'm New in You

"Therefore, we were buried with Him through baptism into death, just as Christ was raised from the dead by the glory of the Father, even so we also should walk in newness of life."

Romans 6:4

Let's start today with this declaration:

I declare today, right now, this moment in time, I desire to change my life. Father God, I ask you to forgive me of all my sins; I repent and turn away from a life of sin. I want to live for You. Come into my life as my personal Lord and savior. Fill me with Your Holy Spirit. I lay down my old ways and pick up the ways of God. Today! Right now! This moment in time, I turn *my* life, *my* desires, and *my* purpose into the hands of Jesus Christ. I will live how the Word directs me to live. I will follow the precepts of God. Lord, you have given me another opportunity to live for You. I thank you for the precious gift of salvation. Thank You for accepting me into Your kingdom as an heir to the throne. Thank You, Jesus, for allowing me to serve and work towards building your kingdom. I acknowledge that in You I live, I move, and I have my being. Today I start my new life in You!

My Time or God's Time

The word "time" is very interesting. We say time is a starting point and an ending point of something or someone. The title of Ecclesiastes 3 is "Everything has its time." My time is notGod's time because I was created in His time. Therefore, the timing of my finite thoughts will never match up with the timing of God.

Today's Devotional:

Allow God's timing to saturate your thinking and your actions. You must allow whatever God must do in and through you to happen in His time without becoming impatient. This might seem to be challenging for some people, but very easy for others. I know for myself, waiting on God was an extremely hard task. Through the process of writing this book, it cultivated my patience through trial and error. Allow God to cultivate your patience. Allow God to prune you in this waiting process. Your prayers and cries have not gone unanswered. You do not have to bargain with God nor do you have to beg Him. Just wait on God's perfect timing. His promise will not go undone. A promise is a promise, especially if it's from Him.

Ecclesiastes 3:1-8

To everything there is a season,
A time for every purpose under heaven:

A time to be born, And a time to die;

A time to plant,
And a time to pluck what is planted;
A time to kill,
And a time to heal; A time to break down,
And a time to build up;
A time to weep, And a time to laugh;
A time to mourn, And a time to dance;
A time to cast away stones, And a time to gather stones;
A time to embrace,
And a time to refrain from embracing;
A time to gain,
And a time to lose;
A time to keep,
And a time to throw away;
A time to tear,
And a time to sew;
A time to keep silence,
And a time to speak; A time to love,
And a time to hate; A time of war,
And a time of peace'

Today's challenge:

Allow every trial in life and every curveball to be overtaken by God's timing. Get it in your spirit that God's timing is the best timing. Don't allow yourself to get frustrated at the circumstances surrounding the timing in which things are happening. Don't get distracted, stay focused. Keep in mind that God's timing is the best timing. God is going to move when He sees fit. You can't rush Him, nor can you manipulate the situation.

Decree with me:

"I will allow God's time to overtake and overshadow my time. I will relinquish my thoughts of time and adapt the move of God's time."

Your Daily Journal Entry

Make Up Your Mind!

While in my daily reading and meditating, I heard God in a small voice said to me, *"Tell my people to make up their minds."* Stabilizing your thoughts stabilizes your faith *"He is a double-minded man, unstable in all his ways." James 1:8*

For many years, I thought being unstable in "ways" meant actions. Now I look at this scripture in a totally different light and I realize James is talking about faith. Listen, you are going to go through some trials in life, but don't worry, these trials come to make you stronger, well-developed, not deficient in any way, and help you obtain patience in faith. You must make a conscious decision, have a made-up mind, and unmovable faith.

James goes on to say that if you don't know what you are doing and you lack wisdom, ask the Father and He will give wisdom it to you; but if you come to the Father thinking you have it all together, and your faith is up and down, you're a person who "worries their prayers" and is like wind-whipped waves.

James is telling us we must *"stabilize our thoughts, which in turn stabilizes our faith".* As we go to the Father, we must *"ask boldly, believing, without a second thought."* It must be in faith that we ask with not wavering (not hesitating, not doubting).

[For being as he is] a man of two minds (hesitating, dubious, irresolute), [he is] unstable and unreliable and uncertain about everything [he thinks, feels, decides]. James 1:8 (Amplified)

Oftentimes when we pray, we become double-minded in our prayers and in our faith. Stop it! If you ask the Father for something, trust and believe He will grant it to you according to His will. If He says no, then trust it is for your good. I know I must be very careful what I ask of the Father because He grants it. Our thoughts must match our faith, and then we will see the manifestation of our prayers...TRUST AND BELIEVE!

Today's challenge:

When you pray today, really trust God. Don't be that double-minded person. Give it to Him. Don't worry about it and don't think twice about it. Pray and leave it in God's hands, knowing He heard you.

Your Daily Journal Entry

Soft in Spirit & Soft in Word

I was an introvert as a child growing up in my mother's house because I was scared to speak what I felt. I stayed to myself and was very quiet until my mother said to me: *"Vioree, it's OK to speak your mind. I need to know what you are thinking and feeling."* Well, she should have never given me that release. However, what she did not teach me was balance in the words I spoke. This got me into a lot of trouble with those that didn't agree with my delivery. Although I may have been correct in what I was saying the delivery was disrespectful. Unfortunately, as a result, I grew up without a filter. As an adult, finding my voice has been one of her greatest gifts to me, it helped me become intentional when I spoke words of healing to those who crossed my path. I'd come to discover the power behind my words. Growing in God allows us to circumspectly view ourselves. When the Holy Spirit convicts us, it is our responsibility to listen.

Here are scriptures I live by which helps me balance what I say (I'm still a work in progress).

Your words:
"A gentle response defuses anger, but a sharp tongue kindles a temper-fire" *Proverbs15:1(MSG)*

Your attitude:

"A scoffer seeks Wisdom in vain [for his very attitude blinds and deafens him to it], but knowledge is easy to him who [being teachable] understands." Proverbs 14:6(Amplified)

I have the power to defuse an argument before it happens, conversely, I can choose to add fuel to the fire and give a sharp word (and my words can be very sharp). I have learned that saying absolutely nothing says a mouthful.

Today's challenge:

Allow the Holy Spirit to bridle your tongue. If you have to give an answer to someone, be mindful of your response. You are held accountable by God for every word that is spoken out of your mouth. Have an attitude of humility in your responses because you can give a soft answer but your attitude can be off, and it will show. Draw people to Christ by our words and actions. Let's grow today!

Your Daily Journal Entry

Beauty

"Do not let your adornment be merely outward—arranging the hair, wearing gold, or putting on fine apparel— rather let it be the hidden person of the heart, with the incorruptible beauty of a gentle and quiet spirit, which is very precious in the sight of God."

1 Peter 3:3-4 (Amplified)

Each of us has our own perception of beauty. What is beauty? Is it a person's appearance? Is it his/her size? Or maybe the way he/she talks? Many say beauty is in the eyes of the beholder. The dictionary defines beauty as *"a combination of qualities that pleases the intellect or moral sense. The quality present in a thing or person that gives intense pleasure or deep satisfaction to the mind, whether arising from sensory manifestations."*

"Let not yours be the [merely] external adorning with [elaborate] interweaving and knotting of the hair, the wearing of jewelry, or changes of clothes; But let it be the inward adorning and beauty of the hidden person of the heart, with the incorruptible and unfading charm of a gentle and peaceful spirit, which [is not anxious or wrought up, but] is very precious in the sight of God.

1 Peter 3:3-4 (Amplified)

The world applies biblical meaning to explain true beauty. You can dress up your outer appearance and speak with great intellect, but it doesn't matter if you are ugly and rotten inside!

"The precepts of the Lord are right, rejoicing the heart; the commandment of the Lord is pure and bright, enlightening the eyes." Psalm 19:8

The heart is where beauty is conceived. Let the beauty of the Holy Spirit shine through your heart. It will, in essence, manifest through your outward appearance. This will exemplify the light, which is Jesus Christ. Your words become gentle in the midst of pain, your appearance becomes brighter in the midst of what seems to be your dark place, and you will carry a glow that will draw souls.

Today's challenge:

Look in the mirror and ask yourself, "Am I the appearance of God's beauty? Do I reflect God's divine beauty?" Ask the Lord to help you destroy every ugly thing contrary to His definition of beauty.

Your Daily Journal Entry

Planted with Purpose

"But indeed, for this purpose I have raised you up, that I may show my power in you, and that My name may be declared in all the earth." Exodus 9:16

A place of silence allows you to hear from God and connect with Him. Silence allows Him to correct you, love on you, and grow you all at the same time. You will always find moments in the scriptures where Jesus went away by himself to pray. Separating yourself from people, social media and the hustle and bustle of life is important to growth, gaining direction and hearing from God. I'm reminded of Job when he prayed in Job 14:7-9:

"For there is hope for a tree, if it is cut down, that it will sprout again, and that its tender shoots will not cease. Though its root may grow old in the earth, and its stump may die in the ground, yet at the scent of water it will bud and bring forth branches like a plant."

There is hope for you. You are planted with purpose! Purpose is the reason for which something or someone exists or is done, made, or used. Whenever you find yourself in a place of confusion; pause, look up, and ask God what is the purpose for what is happening? And what's your purpose for using me for this? Remember, *"All things are created for purpose.* You may feel broken, cut off, abandoned, lost, confused, frustrated, abused, hurt from a loved one's passing, and left for dead with no family or no friends to call on. Is that you today? Or, you may have people all around you and still feel alone! You may have it all but feel empty inside! Then, yes, I am speaking to you!

God is saying:

"YOU ARE MY TREE; allow me to plant you in a place where you can get the amount of sunlight in order for you to grow. I have created you for purpose."

"He shall be like a tree planted by the rivers of water that brings forth its fruit in its season, whose leaf also shall not wither; and whatever he does shall prosper." Psalm 1:3

Just like Job, we all at some point in our lives have to cry out to the Father for help, not understanding why our lives are the way they are. Granted, some turmoil we bring on ourselves but, I assure you that you have hope. God is not slack concerning you, your feelings, your situation, your hurts, or your disappointments. HE'S STILL RIGHT THERE! God has the power to take your wrong, messed-up, jacked-up life and turn them around for your good and His glory! It does not matter what circumstance or condition you are in, He is faithful to pull you out, turn you around, and establish you. Allow

God in your heart by completely giving yourself to Him. Give Him your Mind, Body and Soul and you will never thirst again.
That tree (you) will GROW. If that is you today, please pray with me:

Father, in the name of Jesus, I come to you, asking You to search my heart. I repent right now. Lord, forgive me of my sins. I believe that you died on the cross for me so I may live free from a life of sin. I ask that You fill me with Your Holy Spirit to guide me and help me on this journey called life. Lord, it gets hard sometimes; I am pressured into going backwards. But today I ask that You be my strength and my redeemer. Help me to stay on the path of good. Plant me, establish me, and teach me Your ways and Your precepts so I may be able to live according to Your will and plan for my life. I thank You for accepting me into your kingdom so I may live. Lord, plant me with purpose, in Jesus' name, Amen.

Today's challenge:

Write in your journal what you think your purpose is. Write all your ideas and ways you will walk in your purpose. Be honest with yourself: Have you been walking in your purpose? If not, LET'S GET TO WORK! Begin to plant yourself in God's word so He can establish you in your purpose. This is the only way you will get results. LET'S GET IT!

Your Daily Journal Entry

Strip Search

Examine yourself. Allow the Lord to see into your secret place; that place hidden behind the walls of your smile of sadness, concern, and worry. Come, kneel with me, seeking the Father's face in this silent place where you will find that you are not who you think you are, but, you are who He says you are.

REAL TALK:

Lord, I have experienced a taste of Your glory in my life. I have felt a fragment of your favor and your hand on me. Lord, I need more. I cannot do this thing called ministry, motherhood, relationship, and life without You. I need MORE! Where have I taken You? Into places that you have forbidden. Have I cast pearls among swine? Have I said, "I'm humbled," but deep inside you see pride? Lord search me. As your servant, David sought your face and cried out to You, so do I. I bow to You, Lord, knowing that you give life, and You take life.

"Investigate my life, O God; find out everything about me; Cross-examine and test me, get a clear picture of what I'm about; See for yourself whether I've done anything wrong—then guide me on the road to eternal life. Psalm 139:23-24(MSG)

As you search me, oh Lord, teach me Your ways, Your will, and Your rules for my life. Teach me the ins and outs to live right. Guide my feet to walk according to your plans. I submit totally to You, Father. My flesh, my thoughts, my emotions, my hurts, my gifts, my speech, my home, my children, my relationships, and my assignments are all Yours. They were loaned to me and now I give them back to You. I bring them to the altar. Make new every broken place. Make new every fragile place and make me new in You. Oh Lord, I give my whole being to You, Father.

"God, teach me lessons for living so I can stay the course. Give me insight so I can do what you tell me— my whole life one long, obedient response. Guide me down the road of your commandments, I love traveling this freeway! Give me a bent for your words of wisdom, and not for piling up loot. Divert my eyes from toys and trinkets, invigorate me on the pilgrim way. Affirm your promises to me—promises made to all who fear you. Deflect the harsh words of my critics—but what you say is always so good. See how hungry I am for your counsel; preserve my life through your righteous ways." Psalm 119:33-40(MSG)

Today's challenge:

Take a moment and think about the past year. Can you think of one thing that threw you off course that you desire the Lord to make new? Allow the Lord to strip search your life today and then take the necessary steps to move into your purpose.

Say this:

"Strip me, oh Lord. Search me, oh God, and uncover those hidden things so I may be set free."

Your Daily Journal Entry

Wash Me with YourLove

"Purge me with Hyssop, and I shall be made clean; Wash me and I shall be whiter than snow." Psalm 51:7

As I sat at the kitchen table and sipped my coffee one day, tears began to roll down my face. As they flowed, I asked God to wash me in His love. Many times, we go through life seeking and searching for love, but not really knowing what love feels like. Many of us have seen or experienced love from so many different perspectives. Now we cannot identify what love is or how it's supposed to feel. As you read today, I pray you allow God to wash you with His love. His love is gentle, it's kind. His love will NEVER fail you. His love comforts you in the midnight hour. His love protects and guides. God's love encourages. As you read, allow God to pour His love into you so you may experience His wholeness. This was my cry to Daddy, here's my journal entry for that day.

I had a conversation with God today. As I began to tell Him about all my hurt and why I feel like I cannot move forward, His response was so gentle. He began to remind me how important I am to Him. He reminded me of the times He used me for His glory. He told me I was perfect in His eyes. As I sat there, my heart full of pain and brokenness, He began to speak to every broken place in me.

"Oh, my daughter, you are so precious to me, you have brought me such joy
The homeless have been drawn by My light through you
You have pleased me in your dancing, with your life Why do you hurt by what they say?
Why do you cry because of what they think of you?
You are my perfectly made jewel
You have poured into the souls of My People You have danced until you had no more to give
You have taught until you have no more words to say.

~~~~~~~~

Now rest in me, Daughter Am I not the one you trust? Put your trust only in me.

~~~~~~~~

As you called Me, I was there
As you cried out for Me, I was there
As you wondered when the pain would end, I have never left you.

~~~~~~~~

I love you daughter,
Remember that I was the stone that the builders rejected

~~~~~~~~

I was also talked about by My own
Separated from My home in heaven to die for the sins of this world

They not only spit in my face, but beat me, pushed thorns in my head
Carried the cross that I would hang from for them They pierced me in my side to make sure I would die.

~~~~~~~~~

So, daughter, I know your pain
I know your tears, I once shed those same tears I know that you love Me and I love you

~~~~~~~~~

Know that I will heal you
By My stripes your heart is healed
Know that I will love you when all else fails you Know that I gave you life.

~~~~~~~~~

So, my child, come, let Me hold you until your tears dry up,
Let Me comfort you until you feel no more pain Let Me restore you daughter."
Welcome to the "THE HEART OF A DANCER THAT WAS BROKEN"

As I sat at my computer in tears, I realized I was wounded in battle. I was so hurt, to the point where I cried and did not care who was watching me. I realized healing needed to take place in my heart. I needed to be washed by the love of God. The word of the Lord declares:
~~~~~~~~~

"Wash me thoroughly from my iniquity, and cleanse me from my sin." Psalm 51:2

The sin was not a physical action; it was matters of my heart. When we take our eyes off Jesus and begin to look at who's watching us, we are sinning. When our emotions overtake us and we feel like we are not getting the appreciation from man that we think we deserve, we are sinning. Our God is a jealous God. He wants our *full, undivided attention.* This leads us to...

Today's challenge:

In your prayer time with the Father, ask God to cleanse you of all hurt that you are aware of and unaware of. Many times, we think we are healed from a past hurt, but when faced with a person or situation that reminds us of the past, the thoughts and feelings return. That means you failed that test. You need to be totally healed. Have you ever bumped into an old flame, boyfriend or girlfriend and it caught you off guard? To your surprise, all those old feelings came rushing back. It shocks you because you thought you were healed from that person and the experiences of your past. When you are totally healed, you can see that person and not feel the effects or residue of that hurt. So, let's do this. Write below all the hurt of the past or present that you can think of. Then on the other side, write down the expectations you had for that situation. Why were you hurt from that situation or person? Then write what you learned from that experience. If your answers from your learning process do not match what the word says, you are not healed.

Example: *My old boyfriend was Asian; he hurt me so I will not date another Asian ever in my life.* Now, you know it had nothing to do with him being Asian!

The purpose of this exercise is to get to the root of your hurt and allow God to wash you with His love. When we are truthful and transparent with God, it shows God that we trust Him.

Let's pray:

Father, in the name of Jesus, we come to You today asking You to go deep into those secret places of our hearts and cleanse us of all unrighteousness. Lord, we ask You to search out our hearts that we may be made clean. Lord, we submit to You today all our hurt, pain, feelings of rejection, and feelings of abandonment in the name of Jesus. Lord, we trust You with our issues; we surrender our thoughts to You even now. Father, we ask that You help root out and purge us of every hurt place. Lord, as You are cutting away at our flesh, we ask that You restore to us the innocent love which we were born with. Lord, restore to us the love of Christ Jesus. We understand that it will be a process, but we surrender to the process. We thank You, Father, for taking the time to see about our afflictions. We love You today. Thank You. In Jesus' name, Amen!

Your Daily Journal Entry

CODE RED (Day 1)

"The Lord is near to those who have a broken heart and saves such as have a contrite spirit. Many are the afflictions of the righteous, but the Lord delivers him out of them all.
"Psalm 34:18-19

Many times, when we hear the word "heal" or "healing", immediately we think of physical pain or disease. The next two days, I'm going to share with you about spiritual and emotional healing. As believers of God's word, we go through this Christian walk thinking that because we go to church or we have been saved for more than 20 years, we are OK or we are in the clear. Well, I am sorry to burst your Holy Ghost bubble, but you're sadly mistaken. The day you got saved you became a threat to the enemy's kingdom. For anyone who does not believe that the devil is real, or you believe that you are so Holy Ghost-filled that you are untouchable, please skip past this challenge. I am here to tell you that you are considered "CODE RED" to the enemy and his entire army! The moment you accepted Jesus Christ as your personal Lord and savior the enemy set the alarm and yelled through a bullhorn to his little imps, "CODE RED! WE HAVE ANOTHER ONE! CODE RED"! Just look at it like this: When you are in the hospital and the sound goes out on the loudspeakers, "Code Red," that lets you know that someone is either dying or in critical condition.

This is what happens to the enemy's camp when a soul comes to Christ. He's not only very aware that his time is limited, but he just lost another chance at recruiting a soul to his army. Therefore, he not only panics, but he sounds the alarm to destroy you, to takeyou out by any means necessary.

Today is your news flash. You are not exempt from trouble or spiritual and emotional attacks. Because you made a choice to serve the Father, it is now the enemy's job to "kill" everything God has planned to birth in you, to "steal" every promise God has preordained for you, your family, your ministry, and finally to "destroy" your destiny. As we go through the next two days of devotions, really look inside yourself and ask God what parts ofme need to be healed.

Today's challenge:

Write down the attacks you have faced from the enemy's camp. Write down your deepest hurts and disappointments and pray with me. By the time, you finish these two days, my prayer is that the seed of hurt rooted in you is uprooted by the power of the Holy Ghost.

Let's pray:

Father, in the name of Jesus, I come to You today asking you to hear my heart's cry. See through me and penetrate the secret places of my heart. Lord, I cry out to You as King David did, "Have mercy on me O Lord, for I am weak; O Lord heal me, for my bones are troubled.". I know Lord that through You and only You I can and will be healed — healed from past, present, and future hurts and disappointments. Lord, help me to forgive those who hurt me. Help me, Father, to look past the faults of man as you do, and see the soul, which is Yours. Lord, as I pray for others, heal me. In Jesus' name, Amen.

Your Daily Journal Entry

Code Red (Day 2)

Here's part of my story

*I*t would have been six years that I would havebeen married to my husband, baby's daddy, and friend. God chose to take him home. I thought my world had come to a complete end. I suffered through depression, self-neglect, and thought life was over for me. I went through the stages of grief. I was in denial, and I isolated myself emotionally. I was ANGRY as HELL! No one could tell me about God or what He had done was good or for my good. I was trying to bargain with God, "Lord, if you give him back, I will do this better or I will do things differently.". I then went to my lowest state, which was depression, where I felt like I was going to die. The last stage was acceptance. Acceptance to me is the greatest stage to come to because it is the stage where you have a face-off withGod. God can speak to your spirit. You are in a place where you're not talking, you're not angry, and you're not in denial. You just want answers. Many people die within these stages. But I made it to acceptance!

On the last day of my trip to Las Vegas for a conference, I was in the conference room praying. I heard God say, "Get up and TURN.". Immediately, I got up and began to turn. When I started to turn, I felt kind of weird because I did not know who was watching me, but the more I turned, I felt the presence of God surrounding me. As I turned, I felt a smile come on my face, and I felt God HEALING me. His hand went from the top of my head to my shoulders, to my heart, to my waist, to my legs, and down to my feet. As I turned, I heard people crying in the background, and I heard God speaking to me saying, "I'm healing you. You will not cry any longer. I'm TURNING your mourning into dancing! I'm healing you. I'm healing you". As I turned with a smile on my face, I felt the hand of God cleansing me from the inside out. All my anger, all my sadness, all my depression, all my regrets… God was healing me in that moment as I stood there in tears... I then felt myself drop to the floor, and I heard God say, "No more tears, and sadness.". I laid there and smiled. I knew from that point; the tears had shifted! No more tears of sorrow, but tears of joy! Joy because of what we shared. Joy, because Psalm 30:11 *says: "You have TURNED for ME my mourning into dancing; you have put off my sackcloth and clothed me with gladness.".*

I speak to your spirit today. God is a HEALER! Yes, you will cry. Yes, you will be angry. Yes, you will feel like NO ONE UNDERSTANDS. But just hang on a little while longer. God is healing you. Allow Him to go into the inner places of your heart that ONLY He can reach. God is TURNING that DRY SORROWFUL place into GLADNESS! You will look back and shout because you know, without a shadow of a doubt, that GOD is the ONLY one who brought you out. He knows EVERY tear shed. *Isaiah 53:5 says: "For He was wounded for our transgression, bruised for our iniquities, the chastisement for our PEACE was upon Him, and by His stripes we are HEALED."* Do I still think about and miss my husband Chee- Chee? Yes, I think about Chee-Chee and always will. But now I can smile, cry, and not be sad. Where there is healing, there is freedom, peace, joy, and comfort to know Jesus felt my pain. I know it is ALL in His plan for my life. If you can relate to any part of this story, you are in a "CODE RED" situation. Your process may be different than mine and your experience of needing God's healing may be different from mine. But I pray as you have read these words, that God is healing your body, your mind, your soul, your spirit, and your heart.

Today's challenge:

Tap into those hidden parts of your heart where you may have suppressed so much pain. All of us at some point in our lives have felt a sense of loss, whether it was a loss of a loved one such as a mother, father, sister, brother, child, pastor, or loss of a marriage, church home (lay members), or church (pastors). In the process of grieving, we have all questioned God, asking Him the infamous question, "WHY?" Some of us, even now, have outwardly moved on with life, but secretly are crying tears of sorrow. God desires you to be WHOLE! His desire is for you to live the abundant life. In time, God will reveal His purpose for that loss. We must be in a place to allow God to send the sound "CODE RED" to the ministering, healing angels. God is saying to you today to crack the code, for your healing is RED — the Blood of the Lamb that was shed on Calvary just for you.

Today, I ask you to yell to the father, cry out to Him, and let Him know you are in a state of "CODE RED." When you do, you will begin to feel the presence of God reviving you. He is removing the respirator of depression, sorrow, despair, confusion, rejection, and loss and replacing it with a clean bill of health. If you believe God loves you this much, pray with me:

Father, in the name of Jesus, I bow on humble knees, crying to You, Daddy, "CODE RED". I need You, Father. I need You more now than I ever have before. Lord, I ask that you remove, clean, and purge me of all hurt that is so deep that it has turned into calluses on my heart. Lord, I admit to you that I have become numb to the feeling of love because of the loss I've experienced. Lord, I acknowledge I was mad at You. I was angry at you, and I ask that You forgive me. Lord, I know You are a sovereign God. Your love goes deeper than any valley and spreads farther than any stream. Lord, I ask for Your healing and restoration right now. I want to love again; I want to feel Your healing hand upon me. I believe in Your word in *Isaiah 58:8, "Your light shall break forth like morning, your healing shall spring forth speedily, and your righteousness shall go before you, the glory of the Lord shall be my rear guard."*. Lord, your word tells me that when I call, you shall answer and when I cry, you shall say, "Here I am.". I thank you father for being there every time I called even when I did not feel You. So, Father, on this day, my NEW STARTS NOW. My healing is now in You. Thank You, Father, for Your healing power. In Jesus' name, I pray, Amen. Be healed today.

Today's challenge:

Write down all the *"Code Red"* alerts in your life. Be real with yourself and expound on your fears. When you do, this say to yourself *"My New Starts Now"* No more fear, just faith.

Your Daily Journal Entry

My Desire

"Seek first the kingdom of God and His righteousness, and all these things shall be added to you." Matthew 6:33

This topic might ruffle feathers on many people but hey, that's what happens when the truth sets in. Many people like to put this topic to the side like it does not exist in our homes, our schools, on our jobs, and in our churches. It does exist, and it is very dangerous. It is the "Spirit of Jealousy." This spirit is running rampant in every aspect of our society today. Many may also say, "Well, what does this have to do with my daily devotion to the Father?". It has a lot to do with it. Not only was it one of the commandments set forth from the Father, but also because jealousy is so subtle it can overtake you without you being aware of it. When we hear the word "jealousy" we think to ourselves, "I don't want what they have," or "I am not trying to be like them," or here's one I love, "I know who I am in God.". As I began to study this demonic spirit that is destroying people, I was reminded of the issues that face many of us, not only Christians, but the world, from babies to adults.

Jealousy is an English word etymologically derived from the Greek word zealous, meaning "*vigilant to guard a possession, hostile toward one believed to enjoy an advantage, resentment against a rival or a person enjoying success*".

We may not intentionally covet our brother's possession or his success in life, but secretly in our hearts we go home and say, "Well, why isn't God blessing me that way? I work just as hard as he does.". Or, "Lord, you know my heart's desires. I want a house, I want a marriage, I want a baby.". We must understand that God gives, and God takes away. We do not know the struggles of how that person got what God blessed him or her with. It is very dangerous to wish we had what others have. You see the glory, but you don't know the story. This statement could not be truer. I truly believe what it says in Matthew 25:23, *"Well done, good and faithful servant, you have been faithful over a few things, I will make you ruler over many things. Enter the joy of the Lord."*. This tells me that if I am faithful over the minor things God has blessed me with, He will then begin to increase me. Therefore, be faithful to what God has given you in the season you are in for time He wants you to experience that season.

"Don't lust the things of God, but desire God in His entirety"

When we allow God to grant us the desires of our hearts, it is so much more pleasurable than to lust after our desires. We go wrong when we move before God's time to get what we want, believing in our finite minds we must help God because He is not moving fast enough for us. This is where the spirit of lust sets in. We begin to lust after what we want, and we want it so badly we disregard the voice of the Lord. This becomes sin. That lustful desire can transform into a jealous spirit. You will find yourself saying things like, "How did those people get this, and I have been praying for that for years?" or, "How did that person get to preach before me?". Things we desire become lust when we lose focus of how God wants to bless us. One thing God has revealed to me is that jealousy is often based on an inadequate sense of identity, which fuels depression. If we seek first the kingdom of God and all His righteousness, then all these things shall be added unto us. When we seek God's face and desire Him in His entirety, then God will reveal His will for our lives in His time. When we learn to appreciate the beauty of God within us, we will no longer focus on what our neighbors have, the way they dress, what their ministry is like, or how God is using them. As our desire increases for the Father, our heart's desires will be manifested. In essence, this will combat the spirit of jealousy.

Be encouraged, knowing what God has for you is for you. Stop looking at what others have or how they obtained their blessing; rather, stay focused on being in God's face. Stop desiring the "things" of God and desire to be more like Him. Wait just a little while, sit at the feet of His word, listen to His voice, and seek Him first. This is when God will open His hands and release the blessings from on high. He predestined you before the foundation of the world; He will give you the desires of your heart in His time.

Today's challenge:

Write below all your heart's desires. Write down the things you think you should have at this point in your life and what you think has held you back from obtaining those things, and then pray. Tell God about your disappointments and your setbacks. Let it all out. After you have released those things, ask God what He has for you. Ask Him what His desires for your life are. Remember, what God has for us and what we want for ourselves are quite different. We find that out by being in the presence of the Father.

Your Daily Journal Entry

Covenant Love

"As for me, behold I establish my covenant with you and with your descendants after you" Genesis 9:9

As I was writing this chapter's title, I heard a small voice say, "Read Song of Solomon.". I obeyed and went straight for it. The first thing that caught my eye was the title, *"The Banquet".* I was intrigued, so I continued to read. The writer was very passionate and profound regarding intimacy. I remember thinking to myself, "Wow! I want to feel the intense love this writer is describing.". I remember when Love spoke of me like that. I desire the type of covenant this writer is speaking of again. The next thing that stuck out to me was this:

"I charge you O Daughters of Jerusalem, By the gazelles or by the dose of the field, do not stir or awaken love, until it pleases.
Song of Solomon 2:7

When I read this verse, I began to cry. It reminded me of a time when my heart, mind, body, and soul were pure, knowing not the touch of immorality. Realizing this passion was not the passion of Love but the passion of my uncircumcised heart where no good thing dwelled, I sat and cried. Wanting more from Love, wanting more from this relationship with what I thought was love, my tears were merely drops of liquefied shame. Opening my heart without permission from Love was taking off the garment that cloaked the secret of my existence. Was the covenant broken? Was my shame revealed in the hidden place of silence? The exterior of my beauty was the inner presence of my passion for Love. Had I betrayed Love? Had I failed Love? Fearing the covenant between me and Love was broken forever, tears just fell. Then I remembered that night Love came to me and held me in His arms. The words were simplistic in its speech: "Can you say I love you? Do you believe in me? Do you believe that I love you so much that I died for you? That I got up for you? If you believe this, I will always be right here. I am Love.". As I reflected on those words, I got up and went to the mirror. When I looked in the mirror, I felt myself begin to move to the melody of the air that gushed against the windowpane. As I moved, I imagined I was in the presence of Love. I had on a white, long, sheer, four-layered, flowing dress with angel-wing sleeves. My hair was pulled back in a bun with a hanging white ribbon. I moved to the beat of a harp. To every sound, I moved as if I was floating on air. The clouds held me up, they seemed to be my personal springboard. As I jumped and leaped, I went higher and higher. I danced with such tranquility. At that point I knew Love restored me, the covenant between Love and I was renewed. My soul was at peace with Love.

This story of me feeling like my relationship with the Father had been broken because I was unfaithful to Him; was to show you that

God will never leave you if you acknowledge your faults. He loves you more than life itself. He laid down His own life for you, so there is NOTHING you have done or will do that will make God stop loving you. I felt ashamed; I felt like I had failed. I felt like I let God down after all He had done for me. Yes, the tears lasted for a little while. But He was right there to dry every one of them. He restored me to my rightful place and that is exactly what He wants to do for you today.

Today, right now, this moment was set aside just for you and Love to unite. Your new starts right now. Love is here to comfort you, direct you, and to truly show you what love looks like. The covenant, that promise He made with you, cannot be broken.

Today's challenge:

Write everything you think love should be, what you think love looks like, what love feels like, and how love speaks. After you finish writing, go to *1 Corinthians 13:4-8* (DON'T CHEAT)

Your Daily Journal Entry

GET UP!

"Anxiety in the heart of a man causes depression, but a good word makes it glad" Proverbs 12:25

I dedicate this day to ME! Why did I specifically dedicate this chapter to myself? Well, because one of the things I suffered from in many phases of my life was anxiety, worry, and depression. In the process of writing this book, some mornings it was hard for me to even get out of bed. My body felt like it was its own stronghold. My mind was its own generational curse. The thoughts that plagued my mind were so off from the thoughts and mind of God. Have you ever been there? Well then, this chapter is for you as well.

As we go through our daily lives, circumstances have a way of convincing us that the promises of God that have been spoken over us are far from reality. We are faced with poverty, loss, problems in our marriages, and problems with our children. These issues can somehow overtake us if we allow them to. The Bible says that a "good word" makes a person glad. Many times, all we hear is negativity and what we cannot do or be. Therefore, it is so important to be mindful of what we listen to, the people we interact with daily and what and how we speak to our children. We must remember that our words create our world. Many times, we have to speak over ourselves to remind our inner man the positive things about ourselves.

So, I say to you today, GET UP! Get out of that bed of sorrow, worry, un-forgiveness, despair, depression, and anxiety. There is no failure in Christ. I speak that good word into your spirit today. Romans 8:37 says you are more than a conqueror through Christ who loves you. You are beautiful in Him. He knows the good thoughts He has towards you and that you will make it. As your day gets moving remember to awake your spirit with the word of God. Reaffirm what God says about you. Affirm how He views you which is all in His word. "Failure is not an option for me."

Today's challenge:

Think about those things in your life that bring anxiety, worry, and everything that can give life to the spirit of depression. Those are the spiritual strongholds we will pray against today. Now, you must decide to give those things to Christ and allow Him to work them out. Let tomorrow worry about tomorrow and live today. Let your new day begin with a free mind and a new attitude, giving all things over to God. Take God at His word; He will keep you in perfect peace. Write those things down and pick them up no more. When you find, yourself wanting to pick them up again, go back to this prayer and decree it over your life. Your new day of no worry, anxiety, or depression STARTS RIGHT NOW!

Father God, in the name of Jesus, I come to You today thanking You for allowing me the opportunity to live. I thank You for Your word that brings comfort and happiness to me. Lord I ask that You search out my heart, my dreams and my desires. Lord, You do all things well. I ask You to remove the spirit of worry, anxiety, and depression from me. Lord, I ask that Your Holy Spirit rule over my life. Lord, You know the situations I face every minute of every day; I give them all over to You, never to pick them up again. I thank You for being my safe place, my comfort, and my rear guard. Today I start new in You. My mind shall be in You. In Jesus' name, Amen.

Your Daily Journal Entry

Feelings...Mine are Real

"A fool vents all his feelings, but a wise man holds them back"
Proverbs 29:11

I feel like I am drowning. I know they say God is not a God of confusion, but I'm confused while living in God. I have tried to talk to myself, pray over myself, and even talk to my pastor, but I'm still confused.

I have tried to find comfort in all the wrong places and people. I have called people my friends then, when I leave their presence, I'm as empty as when I came. My feelings, they say, don't matter. So, if they don't matter, why does it seem that feelings are the driving force behind this whole escapade of emotions? Is it to say that when we are in God we should have no regard for our feelings and emotions? Those same emotions that give us the push to love or hate? So why love if we are not to feel? Why care if feelings are not to be taken into consideration?

So many times, I ministered to people telling them, "God never told us to feel.". Is that true? When Jesus was on the cross, He felt the stripes on His back, He felt the thorns in His head, and He felt the nails in His hands and feet! Therefore, if Jesus felt such pain, and

He says to us that we must strive to be like Him, then how can we disregard our feelings?

The belief of not feeling is suppressing your thoughts and emotions to succumb to a statement that's not rightly divided. Jesus felt, so it's true to say we will feel. Why did He put feelings into our five senses if He did not want us to acknowledge them? Feelings and emotions are absolutely 100 percent as important as anything else. They drive us to care, love, hate, cry, scream, and so much more. Feelings and emotions provoke our thought process and our sense of response. It is up to us to bring our feelings under subjection to truth. The truth is Jesus felt pain but continued to press His way to the cross. Jesus felt rejection by those closest to Him, but still said, "I call you friend.". Jesus knew the feeling of betrayal but remained calm in the face of those who betrayed Him. He knew this truth: you are going to have feelings of pain because you are human. But if you keep the faith and go through these painful trials as a good soldier, there will be glory for your pain. Know that your feelings are real and valid, but do not allow your feelings to override truth.

Today's challenge:

Many times, we feel misunderstood. Our feelings are misunderstood and the way we express our feelings to people can be misconstrued. Take a moment and think about some of the things you have had to face in the past six months. Then write down how those things made you feel. Examine those feelings. Then put a scripture on each one. If those feelings do not bring a Godly resolve, then pray and ask God to search your motives and feelings and bring them under subjection to truth.

Your life of feeling bound, broken, rejected, and confused stops TODAY! Your new day of freedom, healing, acceptance, and a sound mind starts RIGHT NOW!

Your Daily Journal Entry

Un-solid Foundation

"You, Lord, in the beginning laid the foundation of the earth, and the heavens are the work of your hands" Hebrews 1:10

There's an unsolid foundation when you build on things not written in the word. Proverbs 21:2 says *"A man is right in his own eyes, but unto God he's a fool."* Well, I must be a fool for building up walls, having a heart of stone and cement-paved mind, all because of an unsolid foundation. Here's my cry to God which was the beginning of establishing a solid foundation within me:

As I move to the next level, I see so much has changed—you, me—our relationship will never be the same. Well, that's what I keep telling myself. As I continue to build on this unsolid foundation—nothing strong, everything weak —and I even look around to see I'm in the middle, should I keep moving forward or should I start over? Mind-boggled, confusion consumes me, living in this repeated cycle of an unsolid foundation. No longer can I stand. I'm in sinking sand, so I fall to my knees and cry out, "Lord, please!"

Tear down the walls of Jericho in my life—everything that blocks me from pressing further in You. Help me see the light. Release me from this cycle of an incomplete mixture which *has been a road paved with lies for my future. People say starting over is the hardest thing to do, but You told me that in You, all things are new. So as this unsolid foundation begins to speak to me again, I lay in your presence so You can chip away at the pieces of this unsolid foundation. You remind me how I got here, building on unsanctified things and unconsecrated dreams. Thank you, Lord, that You were justifying me in the process of this unsolid foundation, knowing I might fall into a state of apostasy.* There are things about this unsolid foundation that you all can't see. It runs deeper than the oceans. *I cry out, Lord, I want to be free! Lord free me from this unsolid foundation that has been built from the sins of my past, the generational curses that have been set up to destroy me, and the insecurities of not feeling good enough. This unsolid foundation keeps echoing in my mind, not allowing me to start again.*

I am reminded that when this unsolid foundation tries to overtake me, You are there to raise up a standard and protect me. I then hear a small voice saying, "Begin again. I have never left you. I told you I will be there until the end.". Now I know that whom You set free is truly free indeed. I remember when you called me royalty. You went to the end and came back again. Then You put me in my mother's womb and shielded me from the demonic goons. You saw me shopping for the material to build on this unsolid foundation—stones and bricks connected to the sticks of hatred and pain. When all the while you were watching and waiting for me to see that you reign.

As I got up from my knees, I felt the weight lifted and my joy restored. God knocked down every wall. He truly heard my cry. He accepted me back in. He once told me in His word that He was married to the backslider. Now, as I look at that sin—never to return—knowing that the thing built on an unsolid foundation begins within.

Today's challenge:

How many of us have tried to build on a foundation that isn't solid, whether it was a relationship, a business, a church, or even soul ties? Let's keep it real, we leave one situation to jump into another one thinking we are healed from the last one, just to find out days, months, or even years later that we were building on sinking sand. So today, think about the things in your life only you and God know you tried to build that were or are sinking in your life. After you finish thinking about those things, ask yourself what was the false identity of that thing. Write it down and find out how you can stabilize that shaky foundation.

Let's pray:

Father, in the name of Jesus, I ask that You touch every person holding this book. I ask You to reach deep into their hearts and reconstruct their unsolid areas, their broken and cracked areas. Father, I ask that You re-cement Your word on the tablets of their heart. When the enemy tries to tamper with the foundation of their heart, Your word will spring up in them and they will say to the enemy, “I am thirsty for the Lord, and it is Him who springs up in me everlasting life.”. I thank You, Father, for your people today. Lord, You have laid the foundation before the world began and I ask that You lay the foundation of Your love in these broken vessels—broken only to be built up by Your love and Your laws in their lives. We thank You, Father for being an awesome Lord in our lives. In Jesus’ name, we pray, Amen.

Your Daily Journal Entry

I Got This

"Beloved, I pray that you may prosper in all things and be in health, just as your soul prospers" 3 John 1:2

Have you ever felt like there was more for you to do in life? Like there had to be more to your existence. I know I have felt that way in many different aspects of my life. I remember when I had my third child, I knew I had to get up and workout to get back in shape for my dance career. I felt so complacent with my life. I was comfortable with being married, going to work, coming home, and living out my daily routine. In all of that, I wanted more—more from God, more from my marriage, more for my children, and most of all, more for me.

I took a step back and began to think about all the dreams and visions I had for myself. I thought about my passion for those things. Then I thought about how my fire had dimmed. Many times, we start out with such passion and drive, but over time it fades away. This goes for every aspect of our lives. We might start out fast, but don't finish. We start a diet and do not see it through. We start out our marriages with such passion for our spouse, then when times get hard, we point out all the faults in that person. We notice all the things we don't like and why we don't like them. I wonder what would happen if we would take all that energy of weariness and turn it into perseverance. We must realize God wants us to prosper in all our endeavors, so the trials that come along with the process of success is meant to make us, not break us. I always say, "How bad do you want it?". If you want something bad enough, you will do what it takes to go get it. Yes, you may get tired, frustrated, weak, and overwhelmed in the process, but at the end of it, you will benefit. Always remember there are benefits to every assignment given to you.

Today's challenge:

Think back on the assignments you have not completed. Or maybe you are the type of person who finishes things but really did not get the lesson in it. Or maybe you are that person who knows it all and is always saying, "I got this.". Well, if any of those is you, get your pen. Write down whichever one I mentioned is you. Take a moment and think back on the things you did not finish and write it. Think back on things you finished and did not see the lesson in it and write it. And if you are the one who knew it all through the process, you missed the real lesson. Now, I want you to go finish it. Think back over the assignment and focus on not what you know, but what you could learn. Look over it and think of what you could have seen in a different way. Remember, there is always MORE to see. There is and will always be a way you did not see before. Allow God to open the eyes of your understanding so you may not be that foolish man who thinks he knows everything!

Always be opened to learn and desire more from God!

Your Daily Journal Entry

Today I Decree!

"Hear my cry, O God; listen to my prayer. From the ends of the earth I call to you, I call as my heart grows faint; lead me to the rock that is higher than I. For you have been my refuge, a strong tower against the foe" *Psalm* 61:1-2

Today we'll decree this prayer over our lives:

Father, in the name of Jesus, I stand in the gap right now praying that You strengthen the saints in this season. Lord, I bind stress in Your name. I bind heart attacks. I bind strokes, depression, suicide, and abuse in your name Jesus. Lord, I ask that You hold back the hand of death, in the name of Jesus. Lord, You are our fortress and in You we trust. Lord, I ask You to block every attack that was set up to take us out while we were sleeping. Lord, it is only by Your power we live, we move, and we are here today. So. Father, I ask You to demolish the enemy's plans and annihilate every evil thing that has taken root to kill, steal, and destroy your people. Father, I thank You for being Lord overall. I thank you for creating us in your image and endowing us with your dunams power. The Holy Spirit has your way in us and through us this day. Create in me a clean heart and renew a right spirit within me. Father your ways are right, and I ask You to be my guide.

Lord, your will be done in my life. I speak life—new life in Jesus' name. Lord, I speak joy back into the lives of your people. Let your power overshadow doubt and fear. Jesus, I thank you for your blood that transforms, heals, delivers, and sets free. In You I have liberty, in Jesus' name, Amen.

Today's challenge:

Personalize your declaration. What are some things that you desire for yourself, your family, and your ministry? Write them down and say them out loud.

Your Daily Journal Entry

VIP Status

Then he turned to the host. "The next time you put on a dinner, don't just invite your friends and family and rich neighbors, the kind of people who will return the favor. Invite some people who never get invited out, the misfits from the wrong side of the tracks. You'll be—and experience—a blessing. They won't be able to return the favor, but the favor will be returned—oh, how it will be returned! —at the resurrection of God's people." Luke 14:13-24

I am reminded of a time when I was reading the Bible and Jesus told me I was *"VIP"* status and accepted. I don't know about you, but I like sitting in the important section. Whether it be a concert, one of my friend's CD release parties, or even in the kingdom of God.

I am reminded of the story in the word of God when Jesus spoke a parable to his followers about a man who was having a party. This certain man invited all the big wigs, so to speak. In our day, the invitees may have been politicians, high-paid rappers or singers, big-time preachers…you get my drift. All the important people reject the man's invitation to come to his party. They made excuses of why they could not attend. So, the host said to one of his servants: "I want you to go out into the streets and I want you to bring in the lower class, bring in the homeless, the less fortunate people. Bring in those who are blind and are sick. Bring me the lame and the crippled." So, the servant went into the streets and brought all those who were requested. The servant reported there was still room for more. So, this "certain man" said to the servant, "I want you to go back into the streets, go into the hidden places of the city, the parts where no one really goes and get those people, the ones who (so to speak) live under the bridges and the ones who are hiding because of their conditions. Bring those people.". Then he said, "I want my place full, for those who were (originally) invited will never taste my food.". The servant went out and obeyed his master, and the house was filled with *"VIP"* guests.

There are two reasons why this story really made a mark on my heart. First, this parable is relevant to today's times. We throw parties, services, and dinners and we invite people we *think* are important enough to come. Many times, when we're going to church, we want to be seen with a *certain* group of people, which we call the *in crowd.* When we host events and parties and the people, we invited who we thought were important don't show up, we get all bent out of shape. We get upset at them and our event is ruined. Have we stopped for a moment to (*oops, here it goes*) check our motives? Have we examined why we wanted and needed those people there so badly? Did we want them there to take a nice picture and say, "Hey, look who was at my event!"? Have we ever stopped to appreciate the ones who did show up? Have we taken a moment to say thank you to the ones who made the sacrifice to come out and support whatever it was we were having? Many times, we overlook those who *really* support and love us for the *fake* ones.

The second reason I love this story is that it shows me that although I came from nothing, Jesus has the power to call me into the high places if I accept Him. This "certain man" went into the low places—the Bible says "highways and hedges"—to look for the ones who were broken, abused, rejected, cast down, distorted, lame, and sick and invited them in. When it's your time, God will raise you up from that low place. When He calls you in, will you hear His voice and accept His invitation, or will you be like those important people who had excuses not to attend the feast of a lifetime?

I'm here to let you know that you are important, you are valuable, and you have "VIP" status, baby! The Father has invited you to a feast that will change your life forever. Think about those men and women from the story who maybe were in the same state you are in now. Maybe you're in physical pain or you may be experiencing a loss of a loved one. Maybe you're confused about a job (you are not paid enough, or you lost your job and don't know how you're going to feed your children). Maybe you feel rejected by those you thought were your family and friends. Or maybe you're in transition in life and you're unsure of the next move. Well, you are invited to be the "VIP" guest. I want you to take a seat at the table the Lord spread out for you. At this feast, you can taste peace and freedom. There is joy and happiness at the table. You're invited to taste water that will satisfy your thirst forever! Come be the special guest today! You're so important to the host of this party. You're invited to sit with the King today...feast with Him, drink of His wine and eat of His bread. When you eat and drink, remember your past is forgiven and you are healed and set free from pain and afflictions. You are so important that He handpicked you before you were formed in your mother's womb. You thought you were counted out by what they said about you, but God was just preparing you for this day, this dinner party. Will you accept His invitation?

Today's challenge:

Think about where you are right now, where you were a year ago, and where you see yourself next year at this time. Write down three things you have accomplished, three things you have failed at, and three things you see yourself doing better or differently. This process is very important to your growth in God because you first must know you're good enough and valuable enough to be a "*VIP*" at God's table. He is preparing you to sit before kings and queens. Your time is now, so start preparing for your invitation to dine with greatness. You're worth it. You owe it to yourself!

Your Daily Journal Entry

Take Action!

"So He said, 'Come.' And when Peter had come down out of the boat, he walked on the water to go to Jesus" Matthew 14:29

*I*n the process of writing this book, I went through a bad experience and found myself going back into depression because of it. I slept in my youngest daughter's bed morning, noon, and night. I got up just to use the bathroom. I did not eat and I barely drank anything. When my children came home from school, I had to fight myself to get up and make them dinner. My son saw that I was not myself and I remember him coming to me one day, sitting on the edge of my bed and saying: *"Mommy, you have to take action. I don't know what's going on, but you have to trust God."*. As he walked out of the room, tears rolled down my face. I thought to myself, "God created me to live and take action.". That was another turning point in my life.

Many times, we are faced with situations that hit us so hard it feels as if it is going to take us under. They knock us off balance, or even rock our world. When this happens, we either have had warnings from God and we ignored them, or we have not sought God's face regarding the situation to begin with. As I was reading the passage in Matthew 14:25- 31, I saw the process from the time the storm came to when Jesus stretched out His hand to save Peter. I noticed when the storm came, Peter said to Jesus, "Lord, if that's you, tell me to come.". This is so profound. We go through things in life and never stop to say, "Lord, what are you teaching me in this process?". Then when God tells us to get up and go, we make every excuse as to why we can't or shouldn't do what He called us to do. As I continued to read the passage, I noticed when Peter got out of the boat, he began to walk on water, but he turned and took his eyes off Jesus. Oh, how this sounds so familiar. We begin what God tells and charges us to do, we start out so excited, and then that *thing* or *person* distracts us from our assignments, and just like Peter, we begin to sink!

I say to you today, don't get distracted. Take action over your fears—fear of failure, fear of succeeding, fear of what people are going to say, and, most of all, fear of your *inner me*. When we give all those fears to God, we can step out into the deep and take action over the assignments God has given us to complete.

Today's challenge:

Think about that thing, person, or place that blocks you from taking deep action. What is it that stops you from stepping out into the deep, taking God at His word, and taking action with your life, dreams and visions? Write it down. Then tackle those things one by one. When you acknowledge your shortcomings or those roadblocks in your life, then you allow God to step in and stretch out His hand towards you to help you with that issue. So, I charge you today: Get up! Step out into the deep and take action!

Your Daily Journal Entry

I Love Me

"Love suffers long and is kind; love does not envy; love does not parade itself, is not puffed up; does not behave rudely, does not seek its own, is not provoked, thinks no evil; does not rejoice in iniquity, but rejoices in the truth; bears all things, believes all things, hopes all things, endures all things. Love never fails."
1 Corinthians 13:4-8

Love.

It's a simple word, but it's packed with so much power and force! I'm not sure if we always understand the meaning of love. We use it so loosely at times, "I love pizza. I love pocketbooks. I love summertime. I love (insert your favorite TV show).". Then we say, "I love God.". Thank God that our love for Him doesn't originate with us, for we'd be in serious trouble. The saying is all too familiar, "I love Him because He first loved me." (1 John 4:19 AMP). We are fully aware that God proved His love for us in that while we still were sinners, Christ died for us. I ask myself often, why is it so hard for us to love one another or to love those who have wronged us and hurt us, or even for us to love ourselves? Why is forgiveness so hard? I find that many of us are hard on ourselves when we make a mistake. We take that same pain and inflict it on those who hurt us. The same force of unforgiveness that we inflict on ourselves, we impose on others. It becomes a cycle of unforgiveness. As the saying goes, "*Hurt people, hurt people*".

It is so important that we get a clear understanding of the word "love", so we have a better understanding of the fullness of God's love for us. How can we respond to this amazing love that was shown to us? What are our actions showing? What are our mouths saying? Are they on the same page? Well, as I began to study the concept of love and the actions that we play in making love an effective language spoken, I realized that many of us say what we don't mean and act out what we want to say. This can be viewed in a positive or negative light. Another thing I hear often is that love is an action word. For example, Jesus died—it was an action to show His love for us. I also see that many do not know how to use their words to express the love they feel. Then there are those who know how to speak their feelings, but do not express their words with action. We need balance.

I believe the word "love" starts with us. When we love ourselves, it becomes easy to show and speak our love to others. We struggle with this because of our past hurts, rejections, abandonment issues, feelings of worthlessness, insecurity, or even abuse. Our parents may not have taught us how to love ourselves first because they were unhappy with themselves. Those are just a few reasons why we may not love ourselves. Let's stop the cycle today. Loving yourself starts first with forgiving yourself of the many things you've done that you were not proud of. Then forgive those who hurt you. I say many times: get rid of the junk and issues of others to effectively overcome your own issues. We must love ourselves enough to say no to others for the sake of our freedom. God wants us to be free to love but guard our hearts. Once again, this requires balance. When we treat ourselves well, we can treat others well. When we serve ourselves (taking ourselves to the movies, going to the spa for ourselves, going to get our nails and feet done, getting our hair done, looking at ourselves and saying, "I love you"), these things validate the love Christ has for us, then we are able to show others how to love, and show them how to love us.

"Love the Lord your God with all your heart and with all your soul and with all your mind.' This is the first and greatest commandment. And the second is like it: 'Love your neighbor as yourself.'" (Matthew 22:37-39)

Over and over, we are told in scripture that to love God is to love one another and to obey His commands. How can we really love our neighbor as ourselves if we *don't* love ourselves? Even more, how can we love our enemies and pray for those who persecute us as we are commanded to do without this love? We can't love our neighbor as we ought until we love ourselves, and we can't love ourselves until we get a divine revelation of the love of Jesus. It starts with us.

"May Christ through your faith [actually] dwell (settle down, abide, make His permanent home) in your hearts! May you be rooted

deep in love and founded securely on love, That you may have the power and be strong to apprehend and grasp with all the saints [God's devoted people, the experience of that love] what is the breadth and length and height and depth [of it]; [That you may really come] to know [practically, through experience for yourselves] the love of Christ, which far surpasses mere knowledge [without experience]; that you may be filled [through all; your being] unto all the fullness of God] ma have the richest measure of the divine Presence, and become a body wholly filled and flooded with God Himself]!" (Ephesians 3:18-19 AMP)

The Father desires that we move beyond a mere intellectual knowledge of His love for us, and through intimate fellowship with Him, *experience* the love of Jesus. We are not our own. Therefore, God's desire is that we reach our fullest potential in love. Such a love compels us to respond in obedience. Such love compels us to receive the love the Father has lavished on us as His sons and daughters, and grown in a healthy, balanced love of ourselves and for others.

Today's challenge:

It may seem crazy, but just do it: Look in the mirror (women, with no makeup) and just stare for about five minutes. Now, repeat after me:

I am beautiful.

I am perfectly made.

I am worth being loved by ME.

I am worth being loved by others.

I forgive myself.

I forgive those who hurt me.

I will not allow my past to keep me bound.

I will LOVE me.

I will cherish me.

I will take care of this vessel.

I will not lie to myself about my pain anymore.

I will allow myself to heal with the truth.

God loves me.

God created a beautiful (son/daughter).

God sees what I have done in my past; I ask for His forgiveness.

I stand in the expectation of the abundant love in Christ Jesus. My new starts now to love with and from a pure place.

Your Daily Journal Entry

Thank You!

"And whatever you do in word or deed, do all in the name of the Lord Jesus, giving thanks to God the Father through Him" *Colossians 3:17*

I am reminded of the story in the Bible when Jesus healed the ten lepers and told them to go and tell the priest what happened to them. What I love the most about this story is that only one of them went back and told Jesus thank you. I often wonder what life would be like without a "thank you", a "hello", or a "how are you", or even an "I love you". Many people live these types of lives today. We go through life overlooking the small things such as a "good morning" which, in essence, may save a life. After my husband got sick the first time, something in me got a wake-up call. Your life can change in a blink of an eye. Yes, we hear of stories but when it is a reality for you, it changes your life. I learned that a simple "hello" or "how are you" can make a difference. Many times, you do not have to speak. You can smile or give a thoughtful wave. It is very disheartening the way society has made it so hard for us to speak to one another or labels us as crazy if we do. I believe that we as humans, first, then as Christians, second, need to set the atmosphere of gentleness, kindness, and peace by a simple "hello" or "thank you", or let's try an "excuse me". I also learned when I wake up every morning and give God thanks for another day—beginning my days with a heart of thanksgiving—it's much easier to smile at someone or give a gentle hello. When we give everything in us back to Christ, it sparks a gentle and kind spirit in us that makes us want to give a kind word. Although this may be the simplest lesson or challenge for the day, I learned it is the hardest for some. Try it!

Today's challenge:

First, give God thanks for allowing you to see another day. Write down ten reasons why you think you should say thank you. Then say hello to five new people today. Not the people that you always speak to, or your road dogs. Push yourself to step outside of the box and be nice to someone. Lastly, reflect on the things you have taken for granted. No matter how big or how small, see how you could have done things differently, and how moving forward, you will have a different response. Write those things down.

Now pray with me:

Father, in the name of Jesus, I come to You today asking You to forgive me for the things I have taken for granted. Lord, I ask that You search out my motives and ill intentions. I ask that You renew the right spirit within me. Father, in the name of Jesus, I am humbly coming to You asking You to pour out Your spirit of love onto me that it may overflow onto every person I come into contact with because, Lord, I know and acknowledge these are Your people. Lord, I come to you saying thank You for all you have done for me.

I thank You for all You have protected me from. Lord, I thank You for keeping me in perfect peace. Father, if this is my last opportunity to speak to You again, here's my thank You. In Jesus' name, Amen.

Your Daily Journal Entry

Freedom

"And you shall know the truth, and the truth shall make you free"
John 8:32

Many of us praise God for freeing us from the things of our past.

We look at others and we see what we could have been or how we could have gotten caught up in bad situations. But do we take a moment to ask God to deliver us from those negative seeds that have been planted and may have taken root in our souls from our past? Selah.

Yes, God rescued you in time but has He delivered you from the residue of that situation? Let me go a step further: Have you asked God to free you from you? Your self- will? Your inner pains? Those things that drive you to hurt others unconsciously? Those words you say that cut people and your response is, "That's just me"? Hmm, I wonder...

Many of us stand free from our past situations but remain bound to our past. Free from the circumstances but bound to those seeds of hurt, abuse, rejection, abandonment, unworthiness, and insecurity. When we are free from those situations but bound to the seeds that were planted to create spiritual chains of bondage, we take those same chains and chain others by our words and actions.

In order to free people, we must first be free. If your words do not match the characteristics of God and His words, then I pray you ask yourself, "Am I free?".

Today's challenge:

Today, I would like you to examine yourself. Examine your past and your present. Listen to the way you speak to people and the way you approach situations. The question is not, "What would Jesus do?" but rather, "Are these the characteristics of Christ?". Many of us do not know the characteristics of Christ so we are unaware that our behavior is not Christ-like.

"Love suffers long and is kind; love does not envy; love does not parade itself, is not puffed up; does not behave rudely, does not seek its own, is not provoked, thinks no evil; does not rejoice in iniquity, but rejoices in the truth; bears all things, believes all things, hopes all things, endures all things." 1 Corinthians 13:4-6

If you find yourself not exemplifying the attributes in this scripture, then you may need to check if you are delivered. Please write in your journal what you want to see different in your walk with Christ, and how you want to be more like Him.

Your Daily Journal Entry

Today I Declare!

I (insert your name here) declare the blessings of God over my life today. I declare every trap that has been set for me is destroyed in the name of Jesus. I will walk in the authority of Jesus Christ to speak my desires and dreams into existence according to the will of my Father, who has all power in His hands. I declare a David warrior spirit over me, my family, and my ministry. I declare a victory anointing over all obstacles I face today. I shall speak words of positivity, which create the manifestation of what has been spoken. I declare what's for me is for me and I shall live to see the promises of God!

Thank You, Father for being mindful of me and my family. I declare, as for me and my house, we shall serve the Lord.

Enjoy your new day in Christ!

Your Daily Journal Entry

Smile

"The Lord bless you and keep you; the Lord make His face shine upon you, and be gracious to you; The Lord lift up His countenance upon you, and give you peace" Numbers 6:24-26

Smiling can give a natural impression of someone that is happy. Fake smiles often can be detected by the lack of zeal behind the smile — it also uses fewer muscles than a genuine smile. You can smile and lack joy. A joyous smile simply means no matter what you are facing, you still have peace because you know all will be well.

A smile not only can help your spirit man, it also helps your natural man. Here are six reasons why we should smile.

- **Lowers your heart rate** – Slows down the heart and relaxes the body.
- **Boosts immune system** – Smiles help the body relax and let the immune system react more quickly and effectively against invaders.
- **Longevity** – The effects of a good smile extend past just the exterior good looks. People who smile more often live longer, too—around seven years longer than most according

to one study. It releases stress, helps the heart, and much more to keep you healthy longer.

- **Kills pain** – Smiling and laughter both have been shown to lessen pain. They release endorphins that lift our moods and act as natural painkillers, too.
- **Increases attention** – Stress limits our perceptions and narrows our attention. Our body kicks into fight-or-flight mode where we can focus on only one of those things. Smiling counteracts this and widens our attention again, opening us back up to multitasking and insights that come from the fringes of our perception and our subconscious.
- **Avoids regret** – We smile to avoid feeling bad for not smiling. Sounds peculiar, but we don't want to hurt people's feelings so we smile when someone shares some story about his/her dog, even if we don't really care. Studies show if we don't smile, we feel regret for failing to do so. This regret brings down our mood and boosts stress hormones.

So, as we see, smiling is a necessity that should be incorporated with our daily lives. *"A cheerful heart brings a smile to your face; a sad heart makes it hard to get through the day," Proverbs 15:13 (MSG).* When we smile and our hearts are glad, we posture ourselves for joy. Joy is much different than being happy. Joy is the essence and foundation of who you are. Happiness is a feeling that passes through your existence. It's simply a temporary feeling with the illusion of the transitory nature of earthly joy. Knowing the difference between the two can help us reveal why one minute we are happy and the next minute we are sad. In all our emotions, joy is the propionate that stabilizes our heart. When we have joy, we will smile through every storm, trauma, heartbreak, loss, and sickness.

Today's challenge:

Today I challenge you to smile. Sounds simple, huh? Well, no matter what transpires during the day, smile through it. Not the fake smile that I talked about. I want you to dig deep and smile. If you find yourself struggling to smile or know deep in your heart, your smile is coming from a place of happiness and not joy, then pray this prayer with me.

Father, in the name of Jesus, I come to You seeking your face for answers. Lord, I desire to experience the fullness of Your joy, the joy that brings back a genuine smile on my face. Lord, through all my hurts, disappointments, and failures, my joy has faded. Lord, You are the one who gives a peace and a joy that surpasses all understanding. I humbly say thank You for restoring to me the joy of my salvation. I smile because You have saved me and have given me a new life in you. Father I thank You, in Jesus' name, amen.

Now smile!

Your Daily Journal Entry

Breathe

"And the Lord God formed man of the dust of the ground and breathed into his nostrils the breath of life; and man, became a living being." Genesis 2:7

As I was writing the final days of this book, I found myself struggling for air. I noticed I would have to go to the back door and stick my head out to catch my breath. I would begin to pray, "Lord, I ask that you breathe the breath of life into me.". That's when it dawned on me that I was having anxiety attacks. I realized the enemy was trying to steal my air. I thought about a sermon my Pastor — Bishop Robert Rochford taught entitled, *"The Spirit of Python is Broken."*. In this message, he said God would cut the head off everything that was trying to kill you. This blessed my life in so many ways.

When you are in the process of an assignment that will bless many, will set many free, and will bring healing to many, the enemy will try to choke the life out of you for that thing not to be born! You will find yourself in situations like mine, having anxiety attacks which I have never had before. Maybe you will have distractions coming from every direction. Or perhaps all you'll want to do is sleep. These are all signs of how the enemy tries to choke you in your birthing process. If he can stop you from breathing life into your project or assignment, marriage, dream, children, or vision, then he knows that he can kill it. Remember, he is doing what he is assigned to do, which is *kill, steal,* and *destroy* everything that was designed for you to prosper and bring glory to God's kingdom.

Today is your new day to take the breath that will rejuvenate, restore, and remind you that you have an opportunity to keep going. It's an opportunity for you to complete your assignment or to get up and start living again. Breathe son; breathe daughter. You have just taken a new breath. Just as my bishop spoke to the congregation that day, here I am speaking to you, *"The spirit of python is broken over your life."*. So now BREATHE!

Today's challenge:

Write down your fears or what you think is stopping you from completing your assignments. Write down everything you think is trying to choke the life out of you. When you are done, write every way you think you can combat those fears. What are some ways in which you can release that spirit of python (besides prayer)?

Let's pray:

Father, in the name of Jesus, I come to You today asking You to breathe the breath of life back into Your children. Breathe into us as you did Adam. Give us life, new life in You. Father, I ask that You cut the head of everything that is trying to choke our dreams, visions, and assignments that will enable us to prosper. Lord, your word tells us that *"above all things you desire us to prosper and be in good health."*. Father, I ask that You touch us with Your hand of life. Give us the desire to live in You. Touch our hearts that have lost the passion to live. Lord in You is the fullness of life— new life. So, I ask that You cut the cord of every dead thing. Demolish the plans of the spirit of python in our lives, in the name of Jesus. Father, we thank You for reigning and ruling over the fowl of the air and the fish of the seas. We thank You for reigning and ruling over every circumstance that comes our way. We acknowledge that you have the final say. You are the beginning and the end, so for this we give You praise. We thank you for another day to worship You. In Jesus' name, Amen

Your Daily Journal Entry

There is Greatness in Your Hands

"Then the LORD answered me and said: 'Write the vision and make it plain on tablets, that he may run who reads it. For the vision is yet for an appointed time; But at the end it will speak, and it will not lie. Though it tarries, wait for it; because it will surely come, it will not tarry." Habakkuk 2:2-3

As I was having my quiet time with God this morning, I heard Him say: "Greatness is in your hands.". I thought to myself, "God, I'm a minister of dance at heart." and He replied, "Go write; greatness is in your hands.". Then it hit me: write the vision and make it plain. I immediately ran to my Bible and began reading Habakkuk 2:1. As I read, the words jumped out at me, reminding me that I have greatness in my hands if I just begin to write.

There's a saying that there are so many dreams and visions in the cemetery. That statement stuck with me because it is so true. Many people died with their dreams and visions locked inside of them. At some point in their lives they lost hope that God would bring those things to pass. Another thing that gets in the way of dreaming big and living it out is a thing called "life." As I sit here and write today's entry, I am reminded of the time I wanted to give up and stop dancing, thinking that my life was useless. Was this thought the manifestation of a word spoken over me from my past or was it a mere feeling that is a stronghold for many today? I had forgotten all the things God said I would do and all of the dreams I envisioned myself doing. They all came to a halt because of the troubles of "life." Looking back, I am glad I had those emotional pauses. They let me know that when crippling feelings try to creep in, I can pick myself up by reminding myself that every word God spoke over me shall come to pass.

I remind you today that you are not forgotten! Remember the time when you used to dream? Remember the time when your visions invaded your head space? Remember when you were excited about life and nothing or no one could tell you that you could not fulfill your dreams? I am here to ignite that passion and fire in you again. Your greatness is in your hands. Write it on the canvas of your mind and dream again. I know doubt tries to bombard you with thoughts of "*How am I going to accomplish this?*'. I will tell you how—WRITE IT DOWN! Put those dreams and visions in the atmosphere and allow the angels to work on your behalf. God is not slack concerning you. He made you for such a time as this. Whatever it is, whether it is a shoe line, a garment line, a book, a store, a ministry, a daycare center, a pet store, or even exterminating roaches—God planted that vision in you for His glory. It is important to remember that your vision is for an appointed time. Just because it is not happening when you want it to happen does not mean it's for naught. Allow God to cultivate it. Allow God to grow you in the vision and dreams that He has placed inside you. When a baby is born, it takes time before that baby can trust another person other than his parents. It takes time for that baby to walk; he holds his parent's hands until he feels secure to let go. Babies get continuing reassurance from their parents to know they are safe. It's the same with us. We must allow Daddy to grow us. We need Him to feel confident that we can handle whatever might come along with the vision or dream He placed in us. Take your time but do your part. So, GET UP!

Write the vision and make it plain for your appointed time to see the manifestation of what God has appointed to your hands.
Remember*: "being confident of this very thing, that He who has begun a good work in you will complete it until the day of Jesus Christ." Philippians 1:6*

Today's challenge:

Go! Hurry, get your pen. Write it down. All those dreams and visions you have buried go get them and bring them back to life on the canvas of your mind. Your greatness is right here and right now. Write down ALL, not some, ALL the things you've always wanted to do, along with all your passions and desires. Write ALL of it. Then make a list. Prioritize the list. Do not think of how it is going to get done. Make the list according to your heart's desire.
Let us pray to seal it in the name of Jesus:
Father, in the name of Jesus, I ask that You hear the hearts of Your people today. I ask that you spark a fire of visions and dreams in the

hearts of Your people. Lord, only You know what happened to make those flames die down, but I ask that You light it again. Lord, I bind the hand of the enemy that is trying to hold, stop, stifle, and kill the dreams and visions of Your people. Lord, we know that what You have spoken over us shall come to pass, so I ask today that You lose the hold in the mighty name of Jesus. Lord, make provision for every vision. Lord gives us favor. I ask You to keep the passion alive as we are waiting for the manifestation, in the name of Jesus. Lord, we believe every word You have promised according to Your riches in glory. Lord, we thank You right now, in Jesus' name, Amen.

Your Daily Journal Entry

Recover

"So, David inquired of the Lord, saying, 'Shall I pursue this troop? Shall I overtake them?' And He answered him, 'Pursue, for you shall surely overtake them and without fail recover all." 1 Samuel 30:8

I love this story of David pursuing the Amalekites. David was a man of high esteem, a man of authority, a handsome man, and a king. He loved the Lord and honored the Lord in all his doings. When David found out that his wives were taken by the enemy, he told the priest, Abiathar, to bring the ephod, and then David went and inquired of the Lord. What stuck out to me in this story is that when we are under attack, the first thing we tend to do is seek answers from our friends and family. We pick up the phone to tell those who we think can or will help us. We also may let our anger out and say many things that we cannot take back. Most of us are driven by our emotions. It's interesting that the first thing David did was put on his holy garments to seek the Lord. I believe if we program ourselves to keep our mouths closed and pray, we will avoid wasted time and misdirected emotions.

It is imperative that you know when you are under attack. More importantly, you must know when to attack back! Some attacks come to knock us off our feet. They come to keep us down and bound for years. When we are under attack, we must be sure to seek

God. He will guide us and deliver us from whatever it is that is trying to oppress us. When David found out what happened, he immediately went to seek the face of God for direction, strength, and courage. When David prayed, God's direction to him was, *"Pursue, and you shall surely overtake them and recover all."*. Not only did God give David direction, but He also gave him a promise. Likewise, when we seek God, He will not only guide us and give us strength, but He will give us a promise. With every attack, there is a promise attached. We must remember that we cannot recover all in our own strength. We need Jesus to go with us or we are destined to fail. It is a trap of the enemy to make us feel like "we got this" when we don't. Greater is He (Jesus) who is in us than he (the devil) that is in the world. Always remember it is in Him that we live, we move, and we have our being. If you allow God to direct your ways in the midst of all attacks, I guarantee you that you will recover all!

Today's challenge:

It's time to take your life back. I know we may hear many preachers say that they don't want what the enemy has stolen because they are more interested in 'the new'. But, I do! If my Father in heaven gave it to me, then it's mine. Peace is mine. Joy, that's mine too. My children—John, Jaida, Camille, and Aleah — are mine. The devil cannot have them. Write down everything you feel you have lost. Pray and ask God if He wants you to have those things. If He does, ask Him for strategic ways to recover all. Trust God when He gives you the answer. Don't get upset if He gives you answers you are not pleased with. In all we do, we want God to have His hand on us while He showers us with His blessings. So, go my brother and sisters, recover all!

Your Daily Journal Entry

Completion

"Being confident of this very thing, that He who has begun a good work in you will complete it until the day of Jesus Christ." Philippians 1:6

FINISH.

That word flows out our mouths so easily, but it is, for some of us, the *hardest* thing to do. I am going to tell you the truth, this book was one of the hardest projects to complete! I had to step back and re-evaluate it so many times through this process. I had so many questions. Was this what God wanted me to write? Is this my assignment to bless the people of God? So many questions of why it was taking me what felt like a lifetime to finish. Some days I would sit at the computer and just stare at the screen wondering why nothing was coming out. Then, when I got up, my mind started flowing with thoughts. That was the craziest thing ever. The closer I got to the end, the harder the fight was to complete this assignment. My Jesus, as I sit back and think about it, I remember calling my mother saying, *"Mommy, it is hard!".* She said to me, *"Baby, yes I know but you have to know it's not for you, it's for someone else, so push.".* I continued to write. At times, I would call my writing mentor, Pastor Rekesha Pittman, and tell her how hard it was to finish, how I feared success, and how I needed help. She would say, and I value these words, *"Writing does not come through*

inspiration, but it comes through discipline. So, sit your butt at that computer and discipline yourself to write every day.”.
would say, and I value these words, *“Writing does not come through inspiration, but it comes through discipline. So, sit your butt at that computer and discipline yourself to write every day.”*

I say all of this to admonish you to complete the task at hand. I know how hard it is to complete an assignment that you do not know where it will take you. You have an idea, but you have no clue what the outcome will be. You do not need to know all the details of what the task is going to accomplish.

Just trust God that if He told you to do it, then complete it. It’s for your good!

Today’s challenge:

I would like you to complete the assignment, PERIOD! Whatever God gave you to do, get it done! It’s a process, so go through the process until completion. I will not tell you that it will be easy, but He will keep you and guide you if you allow Him to. So, I charge you today to rely on God to help you through this. You can do it! Complete the assignment.

Let's pray:

Father, in the name of Jesus, I come to You today, asking You to help me with the assignments You have placed before me. Be my guide and my rear guard. Father I know I cannot complete anything without Your help, so help me Lord. Give me the witty ideas and creative inventions that will push me into my destiny. Lord, I thank You for the resources that are being released on my behalf right now. Lord, thank You for every door that is being opened that no man can shut and for every door that is being closed to protect me from destruction. Thank You in advance for the completion of my assignments. In Jesus' name, I pray, Amen.

Your Daily Journal Entry

You are Awesome

"For you formed my inward parts; you covered me in my mother's womb. I will praise you, for I am fearfully and wonderfully made; Marvelous are your works, and that my soul knows very well." Psalm 139:13-14

As this book ends, and as you begin to decree your future and declare your requests to the Father into the atmosphere, I want you to know you are special to God. He calls you His own. He sent His only son to die for you. Reflecting on this book, I want you to walk away knowing first and foremost that *GOD HAS NEED OF YOU!* There is nothing in your life God cannot handle or heal. There is nothing He doesn't know...You are valuable. God has created you to be great. He has designed you with His hands to do greater things than He has done. You are full of promise and purpose. When you stay in the presence of the king, there is nothing He will deny you, if you live uprightly before Him.

God has designed you to prosper. He has called you and chosen you for this time right here, right now, to live free and to be awesome. God does not desire for any of His children to fail. I wake up every morning and say to myself: "*Failure is not an option*" He has given you the tools to succeed. All you have to do is one simple thing: Pick up the book which gives us new life. In that book is where your

NEW START. Every morning your new day starts with that book. It is filled with promises that will give you hope. It is overflowing with ways to help you overcome. God has equipped you for whatever your plight in life may be. Hold God's word close to your heart, and in the time of trouble, you can speak what God has spoken over you.

My brothers and sisters, my prayer is that you know within your hearts that, as my bishop says, "You have awesomeness all over you". So, walk into your destiny of greatness today!

Your Daily Journal Entry

Declaring & Decreeing

My New is NOW!

I am so blessed that you decided to take this journey with me. My prayer is that you will NEVER be the same. You are new in Christ because you have made the conscious decision to move forward in being the best new you that God created. Remember, He has a purpose for your life no matter what your background looks like, no matter how many people you have slept with, no matter how many times you were married, no matter what mistakes you made, you must always remember you are special to God. He always gives us the opportunity to become new in Him, and your new startsRIGHT NOW! Let's start by making some declarations over your day and your life.

Declarations

I decree that today is a new day with the joy of God that will overflow from the depths of my soul!

Lord, I ask that today You give me the ideas that line up with Your will for my life. Help me to make my life an example of Your living word working in me to advance the Kingdom of God!

- I declare that every good thing You have promised me is MINE in Jesus' name!

- I decree and declare great success over my life, my children, and every person connected to me according to Your will, in Jesus' name!

- I decree and declare, according to your word in Psalms 115:12, that You are mindful of me, my children, and my ministry. I thank You, Lord, that You love me, and you gave Yourprecious son that I may have eternal life in You!

- I decree that today I will write Your vision for my life and make it plain. Lord, today, cultivate that vision and my dreams to manifest in this life!

- Lord, I decree and declare open doors for me today that will create divine connections that will advance the kingdom of God!

- I decree and declare that every plan the enemy has set for me is destroyed by Your power, in Jesus' name!

- I decree and declare that the works of the enemy against me are dismantled by the Blood of Jesus Christ.

- I decree and declare health and wealth!

- I decree and declare wholeness and freedom!
- I ask You, Lord, to awaken every dream and enhance every idea, in Jesus' name, Amen!

- I decree and declare:

TODAY IS MY NEW DAY FOR MY NOW SUCCESS!

My Old Is Gone

My New Starts Right Now!

As my new day is ending, I sit back and see me in a new way. I now know that the old is no more, and my new starts now!

God Bless,

Vioree Brandon

Made in the USA
Columbia, SC
06 February 2024

31600029R00072